Leading Worship

Leading Worship

A Lay Servant Ministries Advanced Course

TAYLOR BURTON-EDWARDS

DISCIPLESHIP RESOURCES

PO BOX 340003 • NASHVILLE, TN 37203-0003
www.discipleshipresources.org

ISBNs
Print 978-0-88177-685-0
Mobi 978-0-88177-686-7
Epub 978-0-88177-687-4

At the time of publication all websites referenced in this book were valid. However, due to the fluid nature of the Internet some addresses may have changed, or the content may no longer be relevant.

The designation *UMH* refers to *The United Methodist Hymnal*. Copyright © 1989 The United Methodist Publishing House.

The designation *URWB* refers to the *Upper Room Worshipbook*. Copyright © 2006 Upper Room Books.

The designation *UMBW* refers to *The United Methodist Book of Worship*. Copyright © 1992 Abingdon.

The designation *WS* refers to *Worship and Song*. Copyright © 2011 Abingdon.

The designation *TFWS* refers to *The Faith We Sing*. Copyright © 2000 Abingdon.

Scripture quotations are from the New Revised Standard Version Bible © 1989, Division of Christian Education of the National Council of the Churches of Christ in the United States of America. Used by permission. All rights reserved.

Library of Congress Control Number: 2013953140

Printed in the United States of America

DR 685

CONTENTS

THOUGHTS ON TEACHING
AND LEARNING

Each of us has a personal and unique learning style. It may be similar to that of others, but if we are able to use a learning style tailored to the way our brain recognizes, stores, and processes information, learning becomes easy and fun, and information is more effectively retained. Think of how you prefer to learn. Perhaps you are a reader. Maybe you learn more easily and efficiently by listening to music, to other sounds, or to voice. Perhaps you learn best in a "hands-on" manner. If the teaching method suits your learning style, you can process and adapt any information quickly. Addressing the educational needs of all students during a session may require you to modify your presentation style.

While lecture alone is the least effective means of presenting material, group activity is one of the most effective. Relational activities in small groups, or sometimes in the larger class context, associate students with different learning styles and thereby offer a way for the teacher to expose students to multiple avenues of learning. Although some sessions will lend themselves to one or more specific learning styles, the instructor can use a combination to address the needs of the students. As teachers, we need to be creative!

Articles and guidelines concerning multiple intelligences refer to the research of Howard Gardner, or the "eight ways of learning." These disciplines can be loosely grouped into three categories, or styles: auditory, visual, or tactile (also known as kinesthetic, as it can involve any form of participatory motion or perceived movement). Here are some activity suggestions:

Auditory
Class discussion
Show-and-tell
Creative rhythms and raps
Debate
Paraphrase or description
Music, songs, or rhymes
Poetry, storytelling, and reading
Word games
Seminars

Visual
Charts and graph
Timelines and diagram
Cartoons and bulletin board
Photographs and video
Posters
Journal writing
Montages, collages, and collections

Tactile
Games and simulations
Puppets
Sculpting
Drama, dance, and role-playing
Singing
Construction
Experiments
Origami and jigsaw puzzles

INTRODUCTION

TO THE COURSE LEADER

This Lay Servant Ministries advanced course focuses on the ministry of the Lay Servant who either regularly or occasionally leads a group, class, organization, or the congregation in worship. The ministry of leading worship is central to any Christian community.

This course is grounded in the classic patterns of Christian worship and the practices of leading worship. By leading this course, you and your class will come to understand more about Christian worship so that you can lead worship with more confidence. You will practice leading worship in a variety of formats throughout this course in order to lead with more competence and grace.

EXPECTATIONS

So that your class sessions can be devoted more to the *hows* than the *whats* of leading worship, you as leader and all the participants should consistently do the following:

1. Complete all the assigned readings before each class session, and bring from those readings a list of the three most important learnings and the three most significant questions the readings raise for you. Each session offers participants time to share and address these insights and questions.
2. Come prepared to embody and strengthen key skills in leading worship. The daily Body Work assignments between sessions help you do this. Practice these each day yourself, and encourage and support your class in doing them daily as well.

3. Come prepared to share with others, be vulnerable to others, and learn from others. Your role as leader is not to be the expert. Instead, you are there to coach others in their learning, answer questions when you can, and point to resources participants can use to learn and grow.

4. Help everyone actively participate in learning and conversation. Lay Servants who are learning how to plan worship will have perspectives and experiences to contribute to the class as valuable as those who have been involved in planning worship for many years. Sometimes those with more experience or stronger personalities may try to dominate the conversation. Your role as leader is to make sure that each person in the class receives the opportunity to share in both small-group and plenary discussions.

DESIGN OF THE COURSE

This course includes ten hours of classroom time (five two-hour sessions), plus additional out-of-class assignments, including reading assignments and practice between sessions. The course may be offered over a period of five weeks, three weeks, or even in an overnight retreat setting. A three-session model might use Session One for an introductory session, Sessions Two through Four for a weekend session, and Session Five for a closing session. An overnight retreat model might begin with Session One in the evening, Sessions Two through Four in the morning and on into the afternoon, and Session Five during the late afternoon and evening.

However you divide the content, begin each session with worship. You will find suggestions for opening worship grounded in the historic patterns of morning, midday, evening (night) prayer from *The United Methodist Book of Worship* in the addendum. Choose the pattern that corresponds best to your class sessions. Morning Prayer is appropriate any time before noon. Midday prayer is appropriate from late morning to early afternoon. Evening Prayer, or vespers, is appropriate from late afternoon to early evening (just after sunset). Night prayer is held well after sundown. These forms of prayer give participants opportunities to take on a variety of different forms of leadership in your worshiping community (greeter, liturgist, reader, song leader, prayer leader). A consistent pattern of worship with a few weekly variations across the sessions will help deepen your sense of being "one with Christ, one with each other, and one in ministry to all the world."

Plan to be the primary worship leader for the first session, and invite the strongest leaders in the group to lead various elements of it with you (reading, praying/singing/chanting the Psalms, leading prayers, leading singing) as their skills and your skills allow. Your first experiences in worship together will set the standard both for future worship experiences and for participants' expectations about how they may lead worship. For the first service, ask those who will lead with you to arrive twenty minutes early to rehearse the service, focusing on smooth transitions between parts.

BASIC RESOURCES

The basic text for this course is *Worshiping with United Methodists: A Guide for Pastors and Church Leaders* (revised edition) by Hoyt L. Hickman (Abingdon, 2007). Each participant will need a copy of the book. It can be ordered through Cokesbury.com or Amazon.com.

The Bible is our primary authority and primary worship resource. Each participant needs a Bible. It will help if participants bring the version they use most frequently where they worship.

Be sure to have enough copies of *The United Methodist Hymnal*, *The Faith We Sing*, the *Upper Room Worshipbook* and *Worship & Song* (if desired) for use during class sessions.

PREPARATION

Before the course begins, make sure all participants have a copy of the required text in order to prepare for the first session.

A letter in the addendum to course participants includes the assignment for Session One. The letter should be sent to participants prior to Session One. You may also wish to provide in advance a list of additional resources such as those mentioned in the addendum of this guide and a display of these resources with ordering information for the first session.

Make sure the space in which you will meet is equipped with a chalkboard, dry-erase board, or sheets of newsprint or a flipchart. Bring a bowl of water, candle, and bell or chime to each session.

Be sure the gathering space is conducive to worship and learning. Consider using round tables rather than rows of chairs. This will help facilitate conversation and small-group activities. Make sure any audiovisual equipment you plan to use is in working order and that persons are present who can operate it.

As the course leader, you should always be prepared. Pray and read scripture daily. Set aside time for silence. Fast if this is a helpful preparatory discipline for you. Ask others to pray with you and for you. Attend to God and be alert to the promptings of the Holy Spirit. Read the required texts and note three insights and three questions before each session that you will share with the class. Familiarize yourself with *The United Methodist Hymnal* (particularly the indexes), *The United Methodist Book of Worship*, *The Faith We Sing*, and *Worship & Song* in order to draw from these resources and help participants draw from them as well.

Practice the Body Work exercises you will lead in each session the night before you are to teach them, and practice them again the morning of the class. This course focuses heavily on the spiritual and bodily practices involved in leading worship. As the instructor of the course, you should set a good example for the entire class. Come to class prepared, and be genuine and gracious to class participants.

Create ways for participants to communicate with you and one another between class sessions. Consider creating a Facebook group or Google+ circle for your class, and encourage interaction by posting class-related questions, insights, links, or helpful resources. This may also be a way for you to share and gain interaction around your three insights and three questions for each session's readings. You might also encourage class members to post their insights and questions for each session. You can create a Twitter account and plan a "TweetUp" once each week. At the very least, collect e-mail addresses and phone numbers of participants, and be sure to contact each class member between sessions. Creating channels of communication and interaction will help class members incorporate the content of the class into their own thoughts and practices, as well as enhance the sense of community and collaborative learning during and beyond class sessions.

Finally, remember that the first session will set the tone for the entire course. Prepare yourself well—body, mind, and spirit. Come to each session gracious and available—both to the Spirit and to participants. Commend yourself, the class, and your time together to the wisdom, grace, and love of the triune God.

ASSIGNMENT FOR THE FIRST SESSION

Read *Worshiping with United Methodists*, chapters 1–2. List three insights and three questions from each chapter.

Ordering Christian Worship— Principles And Patterns

OPENING WORSHIP (20 MINUTES)

Begin each session with worship, rather than introductions or housekeeping matters. Place a bowl filled with water at the entrance of the classroom/worship space. As persons enter the space, greet them by saying, "Remember you are baptized, and be thankful." Using only gestures, invite persons to use the water as they wish. When all have entered and taken their seats, ring a bell or chime to signal the start of opening worship. Suggested forms for Morning Prayer and Evening Prayer can be found in the addendum. You will find additional resources in *The United Methodist Book of Worship*, 568–571 (morning), 574–576 (evening), and 220–222 (music), and in the *Upper Room Worshipbook*, 8–20.

LEARNING GOAL (5 MINUTES)

The goal for this session is to introduce participants to the course and to provide the history and an overview of the Basic Pattern of Christian worship.

COURSE OVERVIEW (10 MINUTES)

After opening worship, welcome everyone to the course and invite persons to share their name, the name of their congregation, and how they are leading or hope to be leading in worship. Thank each person (by name) for sharing. Once each person in the class has shared, present a brief overview of the five sessions of the course.

SESSION ONE—ORDERING CHRISTIAN WORSHIP: PRINCIPLES AND PATTERNS

This session gives an overview of the history of Christian worship, paying particular attention to the development of current United Methodist ritual and ritual resources, the Basic Pattern of Worship, the Christian Year, and the Revised Common Lectionary.

SESSION TWO—THE CHARACTER OF THE PRESIDER: ENERGY, PRESENCE, AND FLOW

This session focuses on the largely nonverbal ways in which worship leaders model the kind of energy needed in each movement and moment of worship and the flow from one to the next. This session specifically addresses leadership in traditional, contemporary, and contemplative/emergent styles.

SESSION THREE—PLANNING AND LEADING ENTRANCE AND PROCLAMATION/RESPONSE

In this session, worship teams will lead and receive feedback on their leadership of the first two movements of Sunday worship.

SESSION FOUR—PLANNING AND LEADING THANKSGIVING/COMMUNION AND SENDING

In this session, worship teams will lead and receive feedback on their leadership of the second two movements of Sunday worship.

SESSION FIVE—PLANNING AND LEADING WORSHIP IN OTHER SETTINGS

Additional patterns of worship are explored in this session, including Morning and Evening Prayer, extending the table, and group devotional acts—praying or singing the Psalms and *lectio divina*.

INSIGHTS AND QUESTIONS (20 MINUTES)

This is the opening work segment of each session. Invite participants to share at least one and as many as three new learnings and one to three questions from the assigned readings, depending on the class size. Larger groups may have time for only one learning and one question per person. Capture these questions and insights on a chalkboard, dry-erase board, or flipchart. This is not a time for discussion. The session itself may answer some questions or reinforce certain insights. As questions are answered, mark them off the "questions" list. There will be time at the end of each session to revisit this list. Be sure to thank participants by name after each has shared his or her insights and questions.

BREAK (10 MINUTES)

KEY CONTENT (40 MINUTES)

Review the "Five Basic Principles of Christian Worship" from *Worshiping with United Methodists*, 17–18.

Review the four elements of "The Basic Pattern of Worship" from *Worshiping with United Methodists*, 21–23.

Walk through highlights of the history of Christian worship up to our present ritual and its use of the Basic Pattern of Worship (*Worshiping with United Methodists*, 23–65). Here is some basic background information that may inform your presentation.

Christian worship has its roots in the worship forms of the Jewish synagogue and Temple. Synagogue worship became the template for the "service of the Word," and Temple worship became the model for the "service of the Table." Until decisions were made by some town councils in Switzerland in the sixteenth century, Christians had always kept these two together— Word and Table—for their weekly gatherings on the Lord's Day.

The first three centuries of Christian worship are marked by great similarity in the *basic actions* of worship (Basic Pattern) and great diversity in the actual texts used in worship. While prayers at Holy Communion were often improvised, the actions of Holy Communion were nearly universal: **take** (prepare the table), **bless** (give thanks for what God has done for us in salvation history and in Christ, and ask the Holy Spirit to make the bread and cup the body and blood of Christ for us), **break,** and **give**.

15

When Christianity became the official religion of the Roman Empire by the late fourth century (375 CE), greater attention was paid to creating and using standardized texts for Christian worship so that the content of Christian worship would be essentially the same everywhere, regardless of the training or skill of the presider. As the Roman Empire itself was already split East and West, distinctive Eastern (Orthodox) and Western (Roman/West Mediterranean) textual traditions began to emerge and diverge from each other. Both traditions still contain the Basic Pattern.

The Eastern Orthodox tradition has altered its texts or emphases little. The Western tradition has undergone two significant changes: First, by the eleventh century, worship had become more penitential in focus. We see this in the greater emphasis given to penitential texts and to the importance of the confessional and in the art in Western churches, most notably the introduction and spread of crucifixes portraying a dead and bleeding Jesus as a prominent image. Second, worship increasingly became less participatory. Most of the service was in Latin, a language fewer numbers of the laity were taught or understood. Moreover, the laity rarely received Communion, owing in part to the penitential emphasis that left the impression that they might have been unworthy to receive. When the laity did receive Communion, they generally received only the bread. The laity was, at best, passive observers of the ritual performed by clergy and monastics.

Reformations beginning in the sixteenth century in the West brought the liturgy and the Bible into local languages and dramatically increased participation in Communion (both bread and cup) and worship generally (congregational singing in the Lutheran church and the Psalter in Reformed traditions). Roman Catholic responses at the time reinforced most existing patterns (the Council of Trent in the mid-sixteenth century). Lutheran worship piety began to shift away from the solely penitential toward Christ as conqueror of sin and death.

Wesleyan Methodism brought rich hymnody to the daily lives of Methodists, though not to official Church of England worship at the time (hymn singing would not be allowed in the Church of England until the nineteenth century). Early Methodists in America began with both society-style worship on Sunday evenings (vigorous singing, exhortatory preaching, and extempore prayer), and Anglican-style worship on Sunday mornings (a service mildly revised from the 1662 Book of Common Prayer with the expectation of weekly Communion). By 1792, a shortage of clergy to serve the growing number of Methodist societies/congregations (average one elder appointed to every twelve charges) led to significant alterations in Sunday morning ritual. As a result, it came to resemble more closely the Sunday night society-style, lay-led service, while leaving the sacramental texts for Communion and baptism essentially intact.

Through the nineteenth and early twentieth centuries, the growth of Methodism in the United States led to changes in official worship resources in an attempt to make worship more "acceptable" to "higher class" tastes. The Basic Pattern became obscured by a variety of "additions" to turn worship into a more inspirational program modeled on the pattern of Anglican Morning Prayer and the revival meetings of the nineteenth century ("entertainment evangelism"). The amount of scripture read during worship was dramatically reduced, and the way that worship was arranged and planned meant that the scriptures chose, and the sermon preached may have had little to do with each other. Sacramental practice was viewed as an addition to the service rather than integrated as a normal part of worship.

Dramatic reforms to the Roman Catholic Church during Vatican II (1960s) were fueled by significant discoveries and scholarship of early Christian worship texts and patterns and led to similar reforms across many Protestant denominations worldwide. The Basic Pattern as embodied in third- and fourth-century texts became the norm for designing official worship texts, and Word and Table became the requirement for Sunday morning worship among Anglicans and Lutherans. It also became the recommended norm among many other Protestants in the United States around the same time, including United Methodists, Presbyterians, and United Church of Christ. The reading of scripture became an increasingly significant part of worship, especially with the introduction and adoption of the ecumenical Christian Year and the Revised Common Lectionary (1992). In 1992, United Methodists became the first denomination in the United States to adopt the Revised Common Lectionary as its primary resource for worship.

The Christian Year was developed to help congregations understand and rehearse the good news of salvation in Jesus Christ and to grow as his disciples. Briefly review the Christian Year as a source for worship planning using *The United Methodist Book of Worship*, 224–26, 238, 269, 298, 320–21, 368, 409–10. Be sure to point participants to the more detailed description of the seasons of the Christian Year found in *The United Methodist Book of Worship*, 238, 269, 298, 320, 368, and 409.

Here is a set of bullet points for your presentation.

- **Advent**

  The second coming of Christ and the culmination of all things in the new creation
  Colors: blue or purple
  November/December 24 (prior to sunset)

- ## Christmas Season

  The Savior is born
  God becomes flesh and dwells among us
  Colors: white or gold
  December 24 (night), January 6

- ## After Epiphany

  The beginnings of salvation
  The early ministry of Jesus
  Colors: green, except for Baptism of the Lord and Transfiguration Sunday (white, or
      gold)
  January 7 until Ash Wednesday

- ## Lent

  The shape of discipleship to Jesus—preparation for baptism and renewal of commit-
      ments to follow Christ
  Colors: purple
  Ash Wednesday until Palm/Passion Sunday

- ## Holy Week

  The cost of discipleship and salvation
  Remembering the last days of Jesus and his crucifixion and burial
  Colors: red for Palm/Passion Sunday through Maundy Thursday, no colors Good Friday
      and Holy Saturday (day)

- ## Easter

  Salvation unleashed
  Fifty days of celebrating the Resurrection and Ascension of Jesus and the coming of the
      Holy Spirit
  Colors: white or gold, Easter Vigil (Holy Saturday night) until Pentecost (red)

- **After Pentecost**

  Living as disciples announcing and embodying salvation

  The teaching and ministry of Jesus (gospel), the meaning and practice of the Christian life (epistle), and the stories of the prophets, kings and patriarchs (Old Testament)

  Colors: green, except for Trinity Sunday, Reign of Christ Sunday (white), and All Saints Sunday (white or red)

  Late May/early June through much of November

Review the Revised Common Lectionary and how to use it to locate readings for each Sunday of the Christian Year. See *The United Methodist Book of Worship*, 227–37 and http://www.umcworship.org. Note that the readings are organized by date for the Sundays after Pentecost.

Below is a chart describing the organization of the Revised Common Lectionary across the three-year cycle that you may copy into a presentation and distribute to your class.

YEAR/ SEASON	A	B	C	Lent and Easter (ABC)
GOSPEL	Matthew	Mark (John 6)	Luke	John
OLD TESTAMENT	Patriarchs and Moses	David	Elijah, Isaiah, and prophets of the Exile	Prophets
EPISTLE	1&2 Cor, Romans, Phil, 1 Thess	1&2 Cor, Romans, Ephesians, James, Heb	1 Cor, Gal, Col, Heb, Phm, 1&2 Tim 2 Thess	l Peter, Epistles of John, Revelation

INSIGHTS FROM THIS SESSION (10 MINUTES)

Invite participants to pair up and discuss what they have learned or had reinforced for them during this session. After seven minutes, invite the pairs to share with the whole group a topic they discussed. Record these on the chalkboard, dry-erase board, or flipchart and discuss them if time permits.

QUESTIONS FROM THE READINGS (10 MINUTES)

Review the questions listed at the beginning of the session. Mark the questions that have already been answered during this session. Answer any remaining questions you can. Then decide and indicate how all unanswered questions will be addressed between now and the next session. Choose a volunteer(s) for the next session's opening worship.

ASSIGNMENT (3 MINUTES)

Body Work: Reading Scripture Aloud

Ask participants to read one of the lectionary texts for the coming Sunday aloud as if they were reading it for worship. Remind them of the basic rule of thumb for reading aloud in worship: Read *half as quickly* and *twice as loudly* as your normal conversational voice, being careful to *enunciate clearly*. Read the passage this way at least once before going to bed at night and again the next morning. Choose a different passage for the next night and the following morning. Repeat this pattern daily between now and the next session.

Read "Attentional Worship," http://umcworship.blogspot.com/2012/03/attentional-worship.html

Read "Bearings in Worship Series," http://umcworship.blogspot.com/2012/05/bearings-in-worship-series-map.html

Remind participants to bring their lists of three significant insights and three questions they have from the reading or Body Work with them to the next session.

SENDING (2 MINUTES)

Sing: "Now, on Land and Sea Descending," verse 1 (*UMH*, no. 685)
Leader: Go now in the peace and strength of Christ.
People: Thanks be to God.

The Character of the Presider—Energy, Presence, and Flow

OPENING WORSHIP (20 MINUTES)

For this session and those following it, choose people to serve as greeter, liturgist, reader, music leader (someone who can sing), and prayer leader. The greeter is responsible for placing the baptismal bowl near the entrance and greeting persons as they enter with the words, "Remember you are baptized, and be thankful." The liturgist begins worship by offering a blessing. The reader reads the scripture and the prayer leader leads the prayers.

LEARNING GOAL (5 MINUTES)

The goal of this session is to practice and receive supportive feedback on planning and leading the first two movements of the Basic Pattern of Worship.

INSIGHTS AND QUESTIONS (20 MINUTES)

Invite participants to share as many as three new learnings and three questions (depending on class size) from the readings.

KEY CONTENT: A WORSHIP WORKSHOP (40 MINUTES)

INTRODUCTION

Distribute copies of the "Observations and Feedback for Worship Leaders" and "What Affects Perceptions of Worship" handouts found in the addendum. Note that this workshop is partly based on "What Affects Perception of Worship" and will be used in Sessions Three and Four to help class members record their observations about how others lead worship.

Walk through and explain "What Affects Perceptions of Worship." You may use or adapt the following script:

In addition to the thoughts and feelings rushing through the minds of people as they enter your church campus and ultimately your worship space, seven major factors will affect how they perceive what is happening in your worship.

Several of these factors are almost automatic and generally unconscious. These include: arrangement; how the space feels; the extent to which persons in the congregation are warm, inviting, somber, joyful, and so on; the energy of the worship space; and the kind of presence embodied by the worship leaders.

Worshipers may become more conscious of the presence embodied by worship leaders—the flow of worship and the way worship is led—particularly when worship does not flow well. All five sessions, along with the readings and Body Work assigned between sessions, are designed to help you improve your skills in leading worship. Your primary role as a worship leader is to use your gifts and role as a worship leader to help worshipers respond to God in the best ways they can.

This session focuses on three of the seven elements that shape perceptions of worship: the different kinds of *energy* involved in the four movements of worship, your *presence* as a leader, and how well you help facilitate the *flow* of worship.

ENERGY

Look at the "Observations and Feedback for Worship Leaders" handout. Under **Energy** you will see an outline that details the kinds of energy needed for a congregation to connect with the purposes of each of the four major movements of worship.

Now, look under **Leadership**. Key to effective worship leadership is for you as a worship leader to **embody** and **model** the kind of energy needed for each movement of worship. This is an important point. Leading worship is more about *showing* what needs to be done by the energy you embody than about *telling* people what to do. *Showing* is primary. If what you show supports what you tell, persons are more likely to hear and follow you.

Let us walk through the different kinds of energy needed for each movement in worship and practice embodying these.

Before Entrance: "Energy Challenge!" Attention and energy scattered in multiple directions

Say to the class, "I want to invite between three and five volunteers to *show* us what their energy is like and where their focus is when they first enter the sanctuary as a worshiper on Sunday." Allow time for several responses from the class. Affirm how each volunteer illustrates the point that we need something fairly dramatic to move a group of people with different levels of energy, thoughts, and feelings to offer themselves to God in worship individually, let alone as a whole congregation. Thank each volunteer by name for participating.

Entrance: Synchronizing the Assembly through Whole Body Actions

In order to begin worship, worship leaders must *synchronize* all their scattered energy and focus and redirect it toward the praise of God.

Worship leaders must embody the kind of energy that breaks distraction and unifies worshipers in body, voice, and spirit in the praise of God. In traditional worship, this may be a brief, powerful call to worship followed or preceded by a processional hymn. The procession of the choir or clergy creates a feeling of forward movement and focus in the entire congregation while the singing of a hymn helps synchronize worshipers' thoughts, bodies, and voices. The energy of worship leaders must be bold, strong, and confident, whether they are leading singing, a brief call to worship, or simply processing down the aisle.

In contemporary worship, synchronization during the entrance happens through what some contemporary worship artists refer to as "the band blast," a loud, strongly rhythmic opening song by a soloist or praise team that invites the congregation to get up and get moving, hands clapping and feet keeping rhythm or dancing in place.

As we have experienced in our opening services for these classes, a period of silence can have an equally powerful synchronizing effect. Synchronizing with silence is often found in more contemplative forms of worship typical of neo-monasticism, some emergent worship settings, Taizé, and, in our case, praying the daily office (Morning and Evening Prayer). Silence as a bodily action can slow the pace of our thoughts and synchronize our breath and heartbeat.

Imagine you are a worship leader for the entrance to either a traditional or contemporary worship service. Stand and demonstrate through your posture and bodily action what this entrance looks like. Ask volunteers from the class to share what they are doing and describe the energy in their bodies as they do it.

WORD/RESPONSE: ACTIVE AND ATTENTIVE LISTENING

There is a significant shift in energy from the Entrance to the second movement: Word and Response. Having offered praise to God, the congregation now turns toward active listening for God's word through scripture, song, and preaching. Ask participants the following questions:

- How would you describe the energy you need to listen to scripture as it is read?
- What kind of energy derived from music or singing helps increase the focus of your attention?
- What sort of energy exhibited by the preacher helps you pay attention during the sermon or refocus your attention when your mind wanders?

Allow time for participants to write and share their responses to the questions and then discuss them with the entire class. Make a summary of the responses participants offer. Ask the class, "If maintaining active listening is the goal, what kind of energy might you need as a worship leader to help worshipers listen attentively and actively?

Ask three volunteers to read one of the scriptures aloud they practiced in their Body Work this week. Keep in mind the questions above and responses shared by the class. Once each volunteer has read, invite the class members to share their impressions.

TABLE: CONFESSION, PARDON, PEACE, OFFERING, GREAT THANKSGIVING, DISTRIBUTION, AFTER RECEIVING

While clergy typically lead the confession, pardon, peace, announcement of the offering, and the Great Thanksgiving, you, as a Lay Servant, may be asked to bring the gifts of bread and cup to the table, prepare the table, serve Communion, or serve at a station for prayer and healing after persons have received the elements. In each of these cases, you are functioning as a worship leader, and the energy you model matters.

If you bring the congregation's monetary gifts to the table, do so with the energy of confident joy. Try to match in energy the speed and intensity of the ushers who are also bringing the monetary gifts of the congregation forward.

If you are helping set the table, be sure to have practiced this beforehand with the presiding pastor so you know not only how she or he prefers the table set but that you set it efficiently with confidence and grace.

If you are serving the bread, look the persons whom you are serving in the eye, break off a piece of the bread, raise or lower it to eye level of the recipient, and place it in their hands as you smile and say with solemn joy, "<u>Name</u>, the Body of Christ given for you." If you are serving the cup, make eye contact with the persons you serve, tilt the cup slightly toward them so there is no need to dip fingers into the cup, smile, and say, "<u>Name</u>, the Blood of Christ given for you." In either case, your energy and body language should exude a confident, joyous declaration.

If time permits, you as the class instructor may want to demonstrate this yourself and invite two or three volunteers to try it as well.

SENDING: ACTIVE/PROPULSION INTO THE WORLD

Immediately prior to the last acts of worship, the energy of the worship leaders shifts again for the sending. The purpose of this part of the service is to send the congregation—having praised God, heard God's word, responded to the word, and been fed at Christ's table—boldly and powerfully into the world as the "body of Christ, redeemed by his blood" in the strength of the Holy Spirit (*UMH*, 10). The energy here is similar to the energy of the entrance, only kicked up a step. Joy, faith, hope, and love should be palpable in the words you say, the gestures you offer, and the way you hold and move your body as a worship leader. While clergy are more likely to offer the benediction, you may be asked to offer the words of sending. Proclaim these words with joy, boldness, and strength. If you are asked to write or improvise them yourself, be brief. Brevity conveys confidence better than many words. Examples include, "Go in peace to love God and serve every neighbor, near and far" or "Go into the world, rejoicing in the strength of the Holy Spirit" or "Let us go forth in the name of Christ."

Invite the class to stand. Model a brief sending for the class, practice it together in unison, then invite two or three volunteers to try it out.

At this interval you may wish to take a short break before the next two sections.

Presence

How does your body feel when you lead in worship? What energy do your bodily actions exude to the congregation? How present are you to God? to the congregation? to yourself? The nature of your presence as a worship leader in each moment of worship has a significant impact on how well the congregation worships.

Ask participants to look at the "Observations and Feedback for Worship Leaders" handout. In his book, *Strong, Loving and Wise: Presiding in Liturgy,* Robert Hovda has identified five key areas in body, mind, and spirit to help worship leaders improve the ways their presence helps others worship well.

Prayerfulness

All worship is either prayer or preparation for prayer. Most of our singing is prayer. The reading of scripture and the sermon are forms of communication between God and ourselves. The Great Thanksgiving is a prayer, and the benediction and sending are prayers of encouragement and strength.

Since all worship is either prayer or an invitation to prayer, it is important that you as a worship leader be prayerful in how you lead. Regardless of context or the type of service you are leading, you must be a person of prayer yourself to lead worship with prayerfulness. Prayerful leadership, as Hovda describes it, is "heavy on awe and mystery, light on answers and recipes" (*Strong, Loving and Wise*, 34). At every point in worship, your role as worship leader is to be focused on the awe and wonder of God as you help worshipers reach and sustain their attentiveness to God. The more you are in "the prayer zone" and the less you are in the "advice zone," both in your words and actions, the more you will be able to sustain your own focus on God as well as that of the congregation.

The extent to which your prayerful presence can best sustain attention will vary from context to context and may vary widely by worship style and genre. The "Attentional Worship" handout gives examples of prayerful worship leadership in three distinct worship settings, each with its own prayer language. (If you have projection and a wireless connection available, you may wish to display this handout on a screen.)

Invite the class to spend three minutes finding three positive examples of prayerful worship leadership in the article. Ask participants to describe the prayer language and prayerful presence each example suggests and how these fit into the context of the service described. Allow one or two minutes for each table to share its observations and answers.

Comfort in Your Own Skin

How does your physical presence as a leader communicate your physical comfort level or comfort in your own skin? Are your bodily actions and language gracious and unrushed? Are your hands fidgety, your movements abrupt, and your eyes constantly consulting the bulletin to find out what happens next? If your movements are gracious and unrushed, persons will sense your comfort as a leader, and they will be more comfortable both with your leadership and their own worship. If your bodily actions and language convey nervousness, uncertainty, or discomfort, or if it seems you are faking emotion, worshipers will be more likely to feel the same in their own bodies, trust your leadership less, and they are not as likely to give themselves to God in worship.

Few of us are ever fully aware of what our bodies are doing as we lead worship. We can benefit from others observing us and offering their feedback on where we seem comfortable and uncomfortable in our own skin. After this course, it may be helpful for you to gather occasionally with a small group of people you trust to view video recordings of your worship leadership and receive their feedback on this aspect of your presence in worship.

Confidence

Confidence is not only about how comfortable you are in your own skin but how comfortable you *appear* in your own skin—how you hold your body, how you make eye contact, and how you use your voice. These factors may vary across different cultural contexts. It is important to know what various postures and bodily expressions convey depending on where you are. In some cultures, a loud voice and quick pace of speech convey arrogance, hostility, or an attempt to deceive, while a quieter, gentler, and more deliberate pattern of speech conveys wisdom. Know the cultural context in which you are leading worship, and adjust your posture, eye contact, and the volume and cadence of your voice to match what that culture is most likely to interpret as confidence.

Care with words

Care with words has three important components. First, words should be used in a caring way, showing care for God, trust, and respect for the congregation. Second, few words may be needed for worship to be effective and meaningful. Third, the worship leader must understand that worship is about our attention to God and the words we use in worship should be chosen carefully, focusing attention on God and not the worship leader.

Ask the class to look at the "Attentional Worship" handout. Invite participants to notice the ways the worship leader uses words in the opening example. What sense do participants get about the presence of the worship leader? Allow time for responses from the class.

FLOW

Flow is concerned with how worship moves from the Entrance to the Sending. Transitions between each aspect of worship should be as seamless as possible. Effective worship leaders guide worshipers through smooth transitions in *actions* and *energy* managed by their own *presence*. Turn to the "Observations and Feedback for Worship Leaders" handout. There are two major categories listed under flow: Minor Transitions and Bearings.

Minor Transitions are the transitions between one action and the next action in a worship setting (Entrance, Word/Response, Thanksgiving/Communion, and so on). These transitions are the changes in the *actions* of worship, and they may require changes in the intensity of energy evoked by the worship leaders (they rarely involve changes in the *kind* of energy required of leaders and worshipers). For example, the transition from the call to worship to the opening hymn is a change in action, from speaking to singing, and may signal a slight increase in the intensity of the energy involved by adding volume, speed, or movement. Bodily action does not change.

For Minor Transitions to be effective, one action must occur as soon as the previous one is complete. Unless there are pauses for silence or contemplation, the next action should start immediately without any "dead space." If you are reading scripture, for example, begin moving toward the lectern during the final verse of the preceding hymn. This allows you to announce the scripture text and start reading as soon as the hymn is over.

Bearings are the transitions *between* the major movements of worship and therefore often involve changes in actions, intensity of energy, and kind of energy. Bearings warrant particular attention from worship leaders. They are like shifting gears in a manual transmission automobile. Effective worship leaders shift the energy smoothly, starting inside themselves, so worshipers may do the same without the shift points distracting from worship.

The Bearings in Worship series from this session's readings discuss in detail how worship design and worship leaders in typical high church, traditional, and contemporary styles may effectively manage the bearings between the major movements of worship.

Ask participants to choose one of the transitions between movements in worship and share examples with others at their table of how they have witnessed worship leaders model these effectively. Allow three to five minutes for participants to share and one to two minutes for the class as a whole to discuss what was shared.

BREAK (5 MINUTES)

INSIGHTS FROM THIS SESSION (10 MINUTES)

Invite participants to pair up and discuss what they have learned or had reinforced for them during this session. After seven minutes, invite the pairs to share with the whole group one of the topics they discussed. Record these on the chalkboard, dry-erase board, or flipchart and discuss them if time permits.

QUESTIONS FROM THE READINGS (10 MINUTES)

Review the questions listed at the beginning of the session. Mark the questions that have already been answered during this session. Answer any remaining questions you can. Then decide and indicate how all unanswered questions will be addressed between now and the next session. Choose a volunteer(s) for the next session's opening worship.

ASSIGNMENT (5 MINUTES)

BODY WORK: EMBODYING ENTRANCE AND PROCLAMATION/RESPONSE

The Body Work for the next session is meant to embody the energy of the first two of the four movements of the Basic Pattern of Worship and the transitions between them: Entrance and Proclamation Response. The four movements of the Basic Pattern of Worship are described briefly in *The United Methodist Hymnal*, 2. *The United Methodist Book of Worship* describes them in more detail (16–32).

Participants should review the readings, the discussion from this session, and *The United Methodist Hymnal* about the energy of the first two movements of the Basic Pattern of Worship—Entrance and Word/Response. Participants should practice embodying the energy of these movements and the transitions between them each morning and night. As instructor, you should offer an example to the class by demonstrating how you might position or move your body to represent the full body energy of the Entrance. You may also show how you would embody the "active, attentive listening" energy of Word/Response. Then show how you would move physically between each of these movements to create a smooth flow. Invite two or three volunteers to demonstrate how they would embody the energy between the two movements. Remind the class that each person is free to and encouraged to embody each of the movements and the transitions between them in her or his own way.

Read *Worshiping with United Methodists*, chapters 5–6,

Review "Attentional Worship," http://umcworship.blogspot.com/2012/03/attentional-worship .html

Review the Bearings in Worship series on The United Methodist Worship blog http://umc worship.blogspot.com/2012/05/bearings-in-worship-series-map.html. Tell class members that they are encouraged to leave comments and questions on the blog.

Remind participants to bring their lists of three significant insights and three questions from the reading or Body Work with them to the next session.

SENDING (5 MINUTES)

Sing: "Now, on Land and Sea Descending," verse 2 (*UMH*, no. 685)
Leader: Go now in the peace and strength of Christ.
People: Thanks be to God.

Planning and Leading Entrance and Proclamation/Response

OPENING WORSHIP (20 MINUTES)

LEARNING GOAL (5 MINUTES)

The goal of this session is to practice and receive supportive feedback on planning and leading the first two movements of the Basic Pattern of Worship.

INSIGHTS AND QUESTIONS (10 MINUTES)

Invite participants to share as many as three new learnings and three questions (depending on class size) from the readings. Note the shorter time for this section, which will allow more time for participants to plan, lead, and receive feedback. Due to time constraints, you may wish to encourage participants to share more of their insights and questions via social media or e-mail between sessions.

KEY CONTENT: A WORSHIP WORKSHOP (60 MINUTES)

INTRODUCTION

During this session and the next one, participants will work in teams to develop a rough draft of a worship service. The service will be built around the Basic Pattern of Worship and the Gospel lectionary readings from any one of the four Sundays of Advent, Year C. Participants may integrate more of the readings from the lectionary if they so choose. Participants will develop, lead, and receive feedback on their rough draft. Remind the class members that they are not expected to prepare a sermon!

In the reading for this session, Hoyt Hickman notes that these two sections vary as to length in an actual service depending on context and the nature of the service. For this session, participants should plan their services five to ten minutes in length. The length of the services depends on the number of teams. If you have two teams, each may prepare a service that is ten minutes in length. If you have four teams, they should prepare services that are five minutes in length. This will give teams sufficient time to present their services and for the class to offer constructive feedback.

TEAM PLANNING

Ask the participants to gather in their worship teams. The size of the teams should be between five and seven persons each depending on class size. Distribute copies of the "Basic Pattern of Worship" (page 61) and "Readings for Advent, Year C" (page 63). Remind participants to pay close attention to the items on the evaluation sheet, and to draw on the identified gifts and roles of each team member as they flesh out, prepare, and rehearse their services. Participants should produce a fairly complete worship bulletin for these first two movements—Entrance and Word/Response—to distribute to all class participants, plus the "mini-service" they will lead (which may not contain all of these elements).

Teams are not expected to offer a sermon (a title and a one-sentence description on the "bulletin" is sufficient). Depending on time, teams may not be able to lead the group in a complete version of their plan. At a minimum, teams should lead the class in the entrance, at least one verse of a song of praise appropriate to their theme and scriptures, the "bearings" from Entrance to Proclamation/Response, at least one scripture reading, and one act of response to the Word (confession of faith, invitation to discipleship, and the prayers).

BREAK

Teams may choose to use part of the break to set up for their service.

WORSHIP AND EVALUATION

Each team will lead the group in worship, using the plans it has developed. The members will begin their presentation by identifying the team's members, the theme for their series or season in which the service occurs, the theme for the service, and some information about the local context where this service would be used. Other class members may note these on their evaluation forms.

After each team has led its worship service, allow two minutes for class members to complete the evaluation forms. Then ask volunteers to share their comments about energy, presence, leadership, and flow with the entire class. Plan to allow about half as much time for feedback from the class as the length of the service itself. If you have a large number of teams, consider running two or more services and evaluation sessions concurrently in different locations, with other teams observing and providing feedback. Allow a brief break between services or service sessions for any final setup the next team needs before beginning its service.

BREAK (5 MINUTES)

INSIGHTS FROM THIS SESSION (10 MINUTES)

Have participants work in pairs with persons from a different worship team. Ask each pair to share one or two points they have learned or had reinforced for them about leading worship during this session. After approximately five minutes, invite the pairs to share one of these points with the entire class. Record the responses so they are visible to everyone in the class and discuss them if time permits.

QUESTIONS FROM THE READINGS (5 MINUTES)

Review the questions listed at the beginning of the session. Mark the questions that have already been answered during this session. Answer any remaining questions you can. Then decide and indicate how all unanswered questions will be addressed between now and the next session. Choose a volunteer(s) for the next session's opening worship.

ASSIGNMENT (3 MINUTES)

Body Work: Embodying Thanksgiving/Communion and Sending (and their bearings)

The Body Work for this week focuses on embodying the third and fourth movements of the Basic Pattern of Worship. Encourage participants to give particular attention to the bearings between Proclamation/Response and Table, Table and Sending, and Sending and dispersion in the world.

Remind the class that the energy at the end of Proclamation/Response moves from congregational prayer toward the multisensory act of congregational praise—the celebration of Holy Communion, which may include the kinetic acts of standing, kneeling, praying, singing, moving, receiving, eating, and reflecting. The Sending often marks a decisive shift in energy from the personal reflection after receiving Communion to corporate "propulsive" energy.

Be sure you let your class know that each person is free to and encouraged to embody these elements and the transitions between them in her or his own way. Invite participants to do a quick run through of the Body Work together, and do it again at their homes near bedtime and again the following morning as part of their daily morning prayer time. As with the previous Body Work exercises, participants should plan to repeat this each night and morning until the next session.

Read *Worshiping with United Methodists*, chapters 7–8.

Review "Attentional Worship," http://umcworship.blogspot.com/2012/03/attentional-worship .html

Review the Bearings in Worship series, http://umcworship.blogspot.com/2012/05/bearings -in-worship-series-map.html

Remind participants to bring their lists of three significant insights and three questions they have from the reading or Body Work with them to the next session.

SENDING (2 MINUTES)

Sing: "Now, on Land and Sea Descending," verse 3 (*UMH*, no. 685)
Leader: Go now in the peace and strength of Christ.
People: Thanks be to God.

....

Planning and Leading Thanksgiving/Communion and Sending

....

OPENING WORSHIP (20 MINUTES)

LEARNING GOAL (5 MINUTES)

The goal for this session is to practice and receive supportive feedback on planning and leading the third and fourth movements of the Basic Pattern of Worship.

INSIGHTS AND QUESTIONS (10 MINUTES)

Invite participants to share as many as three new learnings and three questions (depending on class size) from the readings. Note the shorter time for this section, which will allow more time for participants to plan, lead, and receive feedback. Due to time constraints, you may wish to encourage participants to share more of their insights and questions via social media or e-mail between sessions.

KEY CONTENT: A WORSHIP WORKSHOP (60 MINUTES)

INTRODUCTION

In this session, the class will focus on developing, leading, and receiving feedback on the third and fourth movements of the Basic Pattern of Worship (Thanksgiving/Communion and Sending).

INSTRUCTION: THE FOUR BASIC ACTIONS AND TRINITARIAN SHAPE OF THE GREAT THANKSGIVING

At his final meal with his disciples Jesus *took* the bread, *blessed* it, *broke* it, and *gave* it to them (Mark 14:22). From the earliest times, Christians have patterned the Great Thanksgiving into these same four basic actions: *take*, *bless*, *break*, and *give*.

Taking the bread and cup refers to preparing the Lord's table. Our Anglican and Methodist forebears used the term *offering* to refer primarily to bringing the gifts of bread and wine to the table (not the collection of money). When the gifts arrive at the Lord's table, a deacon, a pastor, or a Lay Servant designated for this task may take them and finish preparing them for the Great Thanksgiving that follows. If the gifts are already on the table before the service begins, a deacon, pastor, Lay Servant, or Communion steward may uncover them at this time. The pastor and those who will serve should then wash their hands.

Blessing is the primary action of the Great Thanksgiving. Led by the pastor, the congregation blesses our triune God for the many ways God has saved us, especially in Jesus Christ. Christians from early on have called this act of blessing by the pastor and congregation a "sacrifice of praise and thanksgiving." That is why we pray, "And so, in remembrance of these your mighty acts in Jesus Christ, we offer ourselves in praise and thanksgiving as a holy and living sacrifice, in union with Christ's offering for us" (*UMH*, 10).

The Great Thanksgiving has a Trinitarian shape. The prayer begins with *praising the Father* (first person of the Trinity). After singing or praying "Holy, Holy, Holy" (often called the *Sanctus*, Latin for "holy"), we continue by giving thanks to the Father for Jesus, the Son. We remember all Jesus did for us, along with his words and actions at his final meal with his disciples. Then we ask that the Holy Spirit be poured out on us and on the gifts of bread and cup. The conclusion of the prayer is a doxology that recapitulates the Trinitarian shape of the whole: "Through your Son Jesus Christ, with the Holy Spirit in your holy church, all honor and glory is yours, almighty Father, now and for ever" (*UMH*, 10). The "Amen" we sing or say together after the doxology is often called the "Great Amen." It is intended to be a joyous and affirmative conclusion to our Trinitarian praise.

During the *blessing*, Lay Servants who are at the Lord's table should pray the same parts as the congregation. At the pastor's direction, they may also raise their hands in a gesture of prayer.

Breaking the bread happens after the Great Amen and the Lord's Prayer. Breaking the bread after the prayer follows the biblical pattern of thanksgiving sacrifices. What is placed on the altar as a sacrifice is broken that it may be shared with those who offered it after the prayer of blessing is complete.

After the bread is broken, it is time to *give* the blessed elements to the people. Jesus *gave* the bread to his disciples after he had broken it. His disciples *received* the broken bread from him. They did not take it, nor did they break it for themselves. This is why the instructions at this point in the service specify that the bread and cup are *given* or *served* rather than *taken* by the people.

The action of *giving* or *serving* should move smoothly but never be rushed. A good rule of thumb is to provide one serving station for every fifty people present.

Lay Servants may assist in serving at the pastor's direction. If there are only as many stations as presiding clergy, the presiding clergy (pastors or deacons) normally serve the bread and laypersons generally serve the cup. Lay Servants may also be asked to assist in resetting the Lord's table after everyone has been served.

Team Planning

Ask participants to gather in the teams they formed during the pervious session. Invite the teams to use the Basic Pattern of Worship and readings for Advent, Year C, the first two movements they developed in the pervious session, and insights from readings and class instruction to develop a plan for the third and fourth movements: Thanksgiving/Communion and Sending.

Remind the teams to pay close attention to the items on the evaluation sheet, and to draw on the identified gifts and roles of each team member as they plan, prepare, and rehearse. They are to produce a fairly complete worship bulletin that includes all four movements to distribute to each class member, plus the "mini-service" they will lead (which may not contain all these elements).

Teams should plan to lead the class through these two movements in no more than five to ten minutes. The services they present should begin with the last action of Proclamation/Response and show the transition between this action and the Invitation to the Table, Confession, Pardon, Peace, and Offering. For the Great Thanksgiving, teams demonstrate what they would do in their roles as Lay Servants during the Great Thanksgiving within their worship context, such as bringing the gifts, assisting with the preparation of the Lord's table, serving, or helping reset the table. They should emphasize the transition between persons receiving Communion and the beginning of the Sending to ensure that energy and attention flow smoothly between these two distinct actions. Groups may wish to consult "Bearings in Worship: Between Table and Sending" (http://umcworship.blogspot.com/2011/04/bearings-part-iii-e-between-table-and.html) as they develop their plans to lead the class through each movement and the transition between them.

Break

Teams may use part of the break to set up for their service.

Worship and Evaluation

Each team will lead the group in worship, using the plans they have developed. They should begin their presentation by identifying the team's members, the theme for their series or season in which the service occurs, the theme for the service, and something about the local context where this service would be used. Other class members may note these on their evaluation forms.

After each team has led its worship service, allow two minutes for class members to complete the evaluation forms. Then ask volunteers to share their comments about energy, presence, leadership, and flow with the entire class. Plan to allow about half as much time for feedback from the class as the length of the service itself. If you have a large number of teams, consider running two or more services and evaluation sessions concurrently in different places, with other teams observing and providing feedback. Allow a brief break between services or service sessions to allow the next team time for any final setup it needs before beginning its service.

BREAK (5 MINUTES)

INSIGHTS FROM THIS SESSION (10 MINUTES)

Have participants work in pairs with persons from a different worship team. Ask each pair to share one or two points they have learned or had reinforced for them about leading worship during this session. After approximately five minutes, invite the pairs to share one of these points with the entire class. Record the responses so they are visible to everyone in the class and discuss them if time permits.

QUESTIONS FROM THE READINGS (5 MINUTES)

Review the questions listed at the beginning of the session. Mark the questions that have already been answered during this session. Answer any remaining questions you can. Then decide and indicate how all unanswered questions will be addressed between now and the next session. Choose a volunteer(s) for the next session's opening worship.

ASSIGNMENT (3 MINUTES)

BODY WORK: PRACTICING PUBLIC PRAYER

During the coming week, class members should practice praying aloud as if they were praying in public. Remind the class that public prayer requires a different kind of "voicing" from personal prayer, much like the public reading of scripture. Public prayer is not personal prayer offered in front of a group. Instead, public prayer involves *leading* a group or congregation in prayer. This is why public prayer often involves a different kind of vocabulary than personal prayer.

Direct the class to the following resources in *The United Methodist Book of Worship*, 20–22, 24–25, 445–47, and 568–80. Remind everyone that posture is part of embodying prayer. Prayers of thanksgiving or intercession may be offered standing, or standing or seated in the ancient Christian *orans* position (demonstrate this posture to the class: palms up, arms extended to the sides, elbows slightly bent). *Orans* is appropriate for all forms of prayer. Additionally, prayers of confession may be offered kneeling, and prayers of blessing may be offered with an outstretched arm. Ask class members to use forms of embodying the prayers that fit the type of prayer they are offering in their daily morning and evening practice sessions. Encourage participants to keep practicing these various postures until they sense of how their body can best offer each posture of prayer.

Read *The United Methodist Hymnal*, 2, 876–79 and *The United Methodist Book of Worship*, 568–80.

Remind participants to bring their lists of three significant insights and three questions they have from the reading or Body Work with them to the next session.

SENDING (2 MINUTES)

Sing: "Now, on Land and Sea Descending," verse 4 (*UMH*, no. 685)
Leader: Go now in the peace and strength of Christ.
People: Thanks be to God.

Planning and Leading Worship in Other Settings

OPENING WORSHIP (20 MINUTES)

LEARNING GOAL (5 MINUTES)

The goal for this session is to learn about and practice leading worship in a variety of settings, other patterns of worship, and multiple forms of prayer. Worship settings for this session include contemporary worship and emergent/interactive worship or house churches. Additional patterns of worship include Morning and Evening Prayer (daily office), group devotions, and sharing Communion with the sick and homebound. Additional forms of prayer include singing or praying the Psalms, centering prayer, *lectio divina*, and *Tongsung Kido* (praying together aloud).

INSIGHTS AND QUESTIONS (10 MINUTES)

Invite participants to share as many as three new learnings and three questions (depending on class size) from the readings.

KEY CONTENT: WORSHIP WORKSHOP (60 MINUTES)

INTRODUCTION

This session's workshop will use the worship planning teams in a different way. In this session, teams will function as practice groups for the various types of prayer and worship leadership that the class will review together after the break. The format for the first part of this session is primarily lecture with opportunity for group discussion in the worship planning teams. If persons are not already seated in their teams, ask them to do so now.

INSTRUCTION: PLANNING AND LEADING OTHER STYLES OF WORSHIP

The patterns for planning and leading worship that this course has reviewed so far can apply to a variety of worship styles. This session will help participants understand how the various patterns of planning and leading worship discussed in this course can be used in two specific styles: contemporary and emergent/interactive worship or house churches. Below is a script you may use or adapt for this session.

Each full service of worship on the Lord's Day by any Christian worshiping community in any style needs to accomplish the following in the order they are listed: enter, hear and respond to scripture, give thanks and celebrate around the Lord's table, and be sent forth to serve. The difference is not in *what* is done but in *how* the congregation offers itself to God and its leaders lead it in doing so.

The principles discussed in Session Two also apply, regardless of the style or context. Energy, presence, and flow always matter. The Lay Servant's role as a worship leader is to lead the people as they offer their worship to God. Maintaining *flow* and attentiveness to the kind of *energy* each movement and each element of worship requires to accomplish its particular purpose is needed regardless of the number of people or the size of the place in which you are worshiping. Your *presence* as a worship leader, in whatever role you may assume, should always embody the graciousness of God in the idiom of the worshiping community.

Here are some additional principles for worship planning and leadership that will help you contextualize the Basic Pattern and basic principles in your particular setting.

Size matters. The smaller the group, the smaller the space, voicing, gestures, "holy things," and technologies required. The larger the group, the bigger the space, the louder the voicing, the grander the gestures, the larger the "holy things," the more intensive use of technologies may be essential. House churches and other worshiping communities that gather in nontraditional spaces often tend to be small, face-to-face, more intimate, and meet in smaller spaces. Contemporary worship with a praise band and/or praise team requires a larger space and more people, not only because of the higher sound level of the band and worship team, but because of the additional persons needed to run the sound and lighting equipment

Ambience matters. Contemporary worship tends to create an upbeat ambience with its music and a challenging message at its heart. Interaction is typically between the worship leader and others onstage or the leader and the congregation as a whole. Many worship leaders in this style tend to speak declaratively and definitively, even if they employ a more casual vocabulary typical of pop culture. If you are asked to lead a service like this and you have not done so before, ask for tips and coaching from other worship leaders in the service so that your voicing, vocabulary, and style of presentation are in sync with theirs.

In house churches or other alternative worshiping communities, the ambience is often more intimate and vulnerable, with a greater openness to leaving some questions unanswered. Interaction here is more personal between leaders and the people, as well as among the people themselves. The overall feel of the service is often more intimate. The language of prayer and ritual used in these settings may be more conversational. Leadership in these contexts requires attentiveness to the presence of the Spirit in the interactions of the people and, at the same time, keeping the service moving forward so it does not devolve into mere conversation. The leader's voice is often pitched, in volume and tone, only a couple of steps above a conversational level, enough to maintain a sense of leadership but not enough to overpower the sense of worshiping as a face-to-face community.

The gifts and skills of the people matter. Worship is not a show put on for an audience. As noted in previous sessions, worship is the work of the people who gather to offer their gifts in the best ways they can. Worship has no predetermined style except for what worshipers in their particular worshiping community offer through their gifts.

This also applies to you as a worship leader. While you should always strive to learn more and improve your skills, you are not expected to lead worship equally as well in every possible style or worship act. Become aware of your own strengths and lead from them. And feel free to say, "Not yet," to any pastor or leader who asks you to lead in ways or contexts in which you feel yourself to be less skilled or experienced.

Purpose matters. Worshiping communities gather for different secondary reasons. Worshiping God is the primary purpose, but what persons seek from their encounter with God may vary widely across size, culture, and style of the worshiping community. Here are four common secondary reasons for worshiping God:

- To *hear a word from the Lord*, word of comfort, challenge, or teaching
- To *abide in the presence*, whether through sermon, sacrament, or song
- To offer God a *worthy sacrifice* through every act of worship
- To discern the work of God in the midst of the interaction and conversation of the people gathered (especially house churches and some emergent settings)

Ask participants to try answering the questions listed below and then to discuss their answers with their worship team.

- Which of these four secondary purposes best describes the community in which you worship?
- Which of these four seems to best describe what you seek in worship?
- What do you believe it takes for someone to lead well in each of these four secondary purposes?
- Which of these four purposes do you feel best equipped in as a worship leader? For which are you least equipped?

BREAK

OTHER PATTERNS AND APPROACHES TO PRAYER AND WORSHIP

DAILY OFFICE

The early church developed two distinctive patterns of worship. One is the Basic Pattern of Worship we have been working with throughout this course. Each of the major services in *The United Methodist Hymnal* (Sunday morning, Marriage, and Services of Death and Resurrection) is built on this pattern.

The other pattern is the daily office, a pattern for household and small-group prayer throughout the day. The word *office* comes from the Latin word *officium,* which means "duty." Early Christians used this word because they considered it their duty to pause several times throughout the day to praise God and offer intercession. *The United Methodist Hymnal* contains orders for the morning and evening offices. *The United Methodist Book of Worship* and the *Upper Room Worshipbook* contain orders for prayer at midday and night also. Night prayer is sometimes called "Compline," from the Latin word *completorium* meaning the "completion" of the day. This service is intended for use by individual persons, families, or groups as they retire for the night.

We have been using Morning (or Evening) prayer to begin each of our sessions. It lends itself particularly well for use in small groups. Its pattern and history connect us to Christians who have prayed this way for seventeen centuries. Many Christians still pray at least these four offices each day.

The basic pattern of these services may be described as Entrance, Readings/Response, and Prayer. These services generally include Psalms and ancient Christian songs, some taken directly from the Bible, called "Canticles." The Song of Zechariah from Luke 1 is associated with Morning Prayer. The Song of Mary (sometimes called the "Magnificat") and the Song of Simeon, both from Luke's Gospel, are associated with Evening Prayer. While our hymnal and *Book of Worship* suggest scriptures for each of these services, entire lectionaries have been developed around these services of daily prayer. One of the most recent is the Revised Common Lectionary Daily Readings, developed by the Consultation on Common Texts as a companion to the Revised Common Lectionary (adopted in 1992 by The United Methodist Church). It may be purchased in book form or downloaded for free (http://www.commontexts.org/publications/index.html).

The daily office may be used for the opening or closing of meetings. The longer services (Morning and Evening prayer) are good for longer meetings, such as church council, spiritual formation, finance, or trustees meetings. The shorter services (midday or night prayer) are better for shorter meetings. Using the daily office in meetings and sharing leadership of them may be an opportunity for you as a Lay Servant to help others grow in their worship leadership in a nonthreatening way.

GROUP DEVOTIONS

You may be called on to lead the devotion for a group or committee meeting. The purpose of a devotion is to attune the group to the guidance of the Holy Spirit for the work they are about to do. Devotions are brief and usually no longer than five to seven minutes.

A common pattern for group devotions is to sing a verse or two of an appropriate hymn, read scripture, offer a brief reflection on the scripture (one to two minutes), and close with a prayer spoken in unison (for example, the Lord's Prayer). You may find it helpful to use the Revised Common Lectionary readings for the past or upcoming Sunday or the Revised Common Lectionary Daily Readings for the day on which your devotion is to be given.

EXTENDING THE TABLE

As a Lay Servant minister, you may be asked to share the elements from your congregation's celebration of Holy Communion with persons who cannot be present on Sunday mornings, the homebound and sick, for example. You are not presiding over or consecrating the elements. You are sharing the elements already consecrated as part of a regular service of Word and Table celebrated in your congregation. *The United Methodist Book of Worship*, 51–53, provides an outline and guidance for visits and a brief order for sharing the gifts of Holy Communion. Note that you do not pray the prayer on page 52. Instead, you proceed immediately from the Peace to the Lord's Prayer while holding the bread and cup. You then break the bread (unless it is already broken) and share it. You may pray the prayer printed in the *Book of Worship* if the other person or persons are able to pray along with you, or offer it yourself on behalf of everyone present. During the blessing, laypersons should say, "Be with *us* all" rather than "*you* all." A complete book and study guide is available for learning more and training others for this important ministry: *Extending the Table: A Guide for a Ministry of Home Communion Serving* by Mark Stamm (Discipleship Resources, 2009).

Ask the class to gather in their worship teams and discuss the questions listed below.

- How do you use the daily office in meetings and other groups that gather in your congregation?
- How might the suggestions offered in this session help you craft or teach others to craft better devotions? What helpful patterns might you suggest?
- How would you describe your experience so far with sharing Communion with persons unable to attend worship?

FOUR PRACTICES OF PRAYER: PSALMS, CENTERING PRAYER, LECTIO DIVINA, TONGSUNG KIDO

For the final part of this workshop, participants are given the opportunity to try four additional prayer practices from *The United Methodist Hymnal* and *The United Methodist Book of Worship*.

CHANTING OR PRAYING THE PSALMS

The fourth-century Christian bishop and theologian Augustine of Hippo is credited with saying, "Whoever sings prays twice." The Psalms are songs that have helped generations of Jews and Christians pray. Whether sung or spoken, the Psalms are intended to be *prayed*, not simply *read*.

No one has access to the original tunes for the psalms. Jewish and Christian singers and composers have developed many ways to sing or pray them over time. Chanting the Psalms is perhaps the oldest continuous form of singing and praying them. This chanting can take many forms. Many Methodist hymnals over the years have set the Psalms to Anglican chant.

The most recent edition of *The United Methodist Hymnal* offers a simpler way of chanting the Psalms. Look at page 738 and notice the text of Psalm 1. Do you see the red dot that appears above some of the words? Now look at page 737. Do you see the five different tones at the bottom of the page? Observe the musical structure of these tones. First there is a whole note. Then there is a red dot over the next set of three notes. The same pattern then repeats with different notes. The whole note is called "the leading tone." You start, or "lead," each line by singing every syllable on this note as if you were speaking it. When the red dot appears in the text, you sing the rest of the line with the final three notes, usually one note per syllable. (Note: If you do not feel comfortable leading the chant, ask someone else to do it. You or another person should demonstrate how to chant the first two verses of Psalm 1 with tone 3. Invite the class to join you in chanting these two verses. Then invite them to chant the entire psalm together.)

After chanting the psalm together, ask participants to share their experience with their worship teams and discuss the questions listed below. (2 minutes)

- Have you chanted a psalm in this way before?
- What was this experience like for you?
- How might chanting the Psalms help you pray them? How might it get in the way?

Point the class to the two other kinds of resources our Psalter includes. There are responses to be sung at the beginning and end of each psalm and at other places designated by the red "R." Responses may be sung even if the congregation speaks the psalm instead of chanting it. The alternation between regular face and boldface print is for praying the psalm responsively, or *antiphonally*. In responsive, or *antiphonal*, praying, the leader prays the lines in regular face and the congregation responds by praying the lines in boldface. In antiphonal praying, the congregation forms two groups, such as the left side and right side, or high and low voices, or the choir or praise team and the rest of the congregation. One group prays the regular face and the other responds by praying the boldface. Before moving on to the next section, lead the class in praying Psalm 1 antiphonally.

CENTERING PRAYER

In addition to leading Evening Prayer or a devotion, you may be asked to lead a group in centering prayer. *The United Methodist Book of Worship* offers three examples of centering prayer (470–72). Some forms of Centering Prayer are active and kinetic, as in the Native American example on page 470. Others are responsive and contemplative at the same time, as with the Asian example on page 471. Others are more individualistic and entirely contemplative, like the example on page 472. In the model on page 472, notice the ellipses at the end of each line. The ellipses indicate a time for extended silence to reflect upon each line of the prayer. Have teams choose one of these three forms of Centering Prayer, select a leader, and practice it together. You may want to ask the teams to spread out in different locations so they do not disturb one another.

LECTIO DIVINA

Lectio divina (Latin for "divine reading") is a way of reading scripture aloud in a group setting, reflecting on it, and sharing what is heard among group members. In *lectio divina* a scripture passage is selected and read aloud three times. Before the first reading, the group is asked to listen for what captures their attention. A period of silence is observed for persons to reflect. Before the second reading, the group members are invited to listen to what the Holy Spirit may be saying to them by reflecting on what captured their attention during the first reading. A period of silence is observed a second time for persons to reflect on the Spirit's direction. Before the third reading, the group members are invited to consider how they might respond to what the Spirit has shown or asked of them. A final period of silence follows for persons to write down or make their commitment firm. Following the period of silence, persons are invited to share what captured their attention in the scripture passage, what they heard, and what they will do in response. This is a time for reporting and testimony, not group discussion.

Invite participants to remain in their worship teams and spend a few minutes practicing *lectio divina* together with the scripture for this session, either John 20:19-29 (evening) or John 21:1-14 (morning).

TONGSUNG KIDO (PRAYING ALOUD TOGETHER)

While the name of this method of prayer is Korean, in reality this is a typical way of praying in many Asian, Hispanic, and Latino Christian communities. Lay Servants may be asked to lead this type of prayer in some contexts.

Tongsung Kido is designed for the prayers of the people. It is a way for persons to pray actively, aloud, and simultaneously. As the description in the *Book of Worship* (page 446) indicates, the prayer leader announces a topic on which the group will pray. Persons then offer their prayers around that topic aloud and simultaneously. Praying this way may not come naturally to those who are accustomed to a single voice leading the entire group in prayer or waiting for others to pray before speaking. It may be helpful to think of this in terms of a group of people from different cultures praying the Lord's Prayer aloud and all at once in their native languages. Before the break, lead the class in *Tongsung Kido* using the intercessory prompts from the opening worship of each session (*UMH*, no. 877 or *UMH*, no. 879).

BREAK (5 MINUTES)

INSIGHTS FROM THIS SESSION (5 MINUTES)

Have participants work in pairs with persons from a different worship team. Ask each pair to share one or two points they have learned or had reinforced for them about leading worship during this session. After approximately five minutes, invite the pairs to share one of these points with the entire class. Record the responses so they are visible to everyone in the class and discuss them if time permits.

QUESTIONS FROM THE READINGS (5 MINUTES)

Review the questions listed at the beginning of the session. Mark the questions that have already been answered during this session. Answer any remaining questions you can.

COURSE EVALUATION (5 MINUTES)

Ask participants to respond to the open-ended questions list below. You may wish to write these on a chalkboard, dry-erase board, or flipchart so they are visible to everyone in the class, or you can prepare handouts with space for participants to write their answers.

- The three most important things I have learned in this course are. . .
- I wish the course had included more. . .
- I wish the course had included less. . .

SENDING (5 MINUTES)

Sing: "Benediction Hymn" (*WS*, no. 3182)
Leader: Go now in the peace and strength of Christ.
People: Thanks be to God.

Addendum

LETTER TO THE COURSE PARTICIPANT

This Lay Servant Ministries advanced course focuses on the ministry of the Lay Servant who either regularly or occasionally leads a group, class, organization, or the congregation in worship. The ministry of leading worship is central to any Christian community.

This course is grounded in the classic patterns of Christian worship and the practices of leading worship. By taking this course, you will learn more about Christian worship in order to lead with more confidence. You will also practice leading worship in a variety of formats throughout this course so that you may lead with more competence and grace.

EXPECTATIONS

So that your class sessions can be devoted more to the *hows* than the *whats* of leading worship, you should consistently do the following:

1. Complete all the assigned readings before each class session, and glean from those readings a list of the three most important learnings and the three most significant questions they raised for you. Each session is designed to offer the class time to share and address these insights and questions.
2. Come ready to embody and strengthen key *skills* in leading worship. The daily Body Work assignments between sessions are there to help you do this. Do these each day.
3. Come ready to share with others, be vulnerable to others, and learn from others.

DESIGN OF THE COURSE

This course includes ten hours of classroom time divided into five two-hour sessions, plus additional out-of-class assignments, including reading assignments and practice between sessions. Each session will begin with worship and follow the same basic rubric.

BASIC RESOURCES

The basic text for this course is *Worshiping with United Methodists: A Guide for Pastors and Church Leaders* (revised edition) by Hoyt L. Hickman (Abingdon, 2007). Each participant will need a copy of the book. It can be ordered through Cokesbury.com or Amazon.com.

The Bible is our primary authority and our primary worship resource. Each participant needs a Bible. It is most helpful if participants bring the version used most frequently where they worship regularly.

ASSIGNMENT FOR THE FIRST SESSION

Read *Worshiping with United Methodists*, chapters 1–2. List three insights and three questions from each chapter.

WORSHIP RESOURCES

EVENING PRAYER

Ring a bell or chime to signal to the class that it is time to begin. Then enter into a period of silence.

Continue in silence, lighting a candle that is clearly visible to everyone in the room.

The silence is broken by the call to worship.

Leader: Light and peace in Jesus Christ.
All: Thanks be to God.

If desired, candles may be distributed to participants to light during the singing of the evening hymn. Ask the class to stand for the hymn.

Evening Hymn: For Sessions One, Two, and Three, choose from "Christ, Mighty Savior" (*UMH*, no. 684), "O Gladsome Light" (*UMH*, no. 686), or "Now It Is Evening" (*TFWS*, no. 2187). For Session Four sing, "The Day Thou Gavest, Lord, Is Ended" (*UMH*, no. 690). For Session Five, for session Five sing, "Creator of the Stars of Night" (*UMH*, no. 692). This ancient tune may be unfamiliar. If so, you may wish to substitute another tune in Long Meter (LM). Tallis Canon is also appropriate (*UMH*, no. 682). For more information, see the Metrical Index (*UMH*, pages 926–27).

After the singing of the hymn, signal participants to sit.

Scripture

> Session One: Genesis 1:1-5
> Session Two: Genesis 1:14-19

Session Three: Exodus 13:17-22
Session Four: Luke 24:28-35
Session Five: John 20:19-29

Silence (2 minutes)

Ask participants to stand for the song and the prayers.

Song (The Canticle of Mary is customary, *UMH*, no. 199 or 200)

Prayers of the People (Spoken UMH, no. 879; Sung *TFWS*, no. 2201)

The instructor leads the intercessions for the opening session. Course participants will lead in succeeding sessions. If you choose to sing, do so in a "normal," almost "spoken" register. Participants may remain silent except responses, or they may lift up names of persons or situations related to each petition. Conclude the intercessions with, "for the forgiveness of our sins."

Silence (1 minute)

Leader: Hear the good news. If we confess our sins, God is faithful and just and will forgive us our sins and cleanse us from all unrighteousness. In the name of Jesus Christ, we are forgiven.
People: In the name of Jesus Christ, we are all forgiven.
All: Glory to God, *Amen.*

Lord's Prayer

Blessing

Leader: May the grace of Jesus Christ be with us this night and always.
People: Thanks be to God.

The Peace

MORNING PRAYER

Place a bowl of water (the baptismal bowl) at the entrance of the worship/class space. As persons enter, the greeter says to them, "<u>Name</u>, remember you are baptized, and be thankful." A bell sounds, inviting silence. A candle is then lit, and the liturgist interrupts the silence with the call to worship.

Liturgist: O Lord, open our lips.
All: And our mouths shall declare your praise.

The song leader invites everyone to stand. During the first session, the song leader sings the first verse of the hymn below, invites the class to sing the first verse, and then everyone sings the hymn in its entirety. After the final verse, repeat the opening refrain twice.

O God, Open Our Lips

WORDS and MUSIC: Taylor Burton-Edwards, Based on Psalms 95 and 98

Scripture

Session One: Deuteronomy 4:1-9
Session Two: Isaiah 12:2-6
Session Three: Isaiah 55:6-11
Session Four: John 1:1-5, 9-14
Session Five: John 21:1-14

Silence (2 minutes)

Song (standing)

Session One: Canticle of Zechariah (*UMH*, no. 208)
Session Two: Canticle of Praise to God (*UMH*, no. 91)
Session Three: Canticle of God's Glory (*UMH*, no. 82 or 83)
Session Four: Canticle of the Holy Trinity (*UMH*, no. 80)
Session Five: Canticle of Thanksgiving (*UMH*, no. 74)

Prayer (remain standing)

Prayers of the People (Spoken *UMH*, no. 877; Sung *TFWS*, no. 2201)

Lead the prayer intercessions yourself, or invite another person to lead them. If you choose an arrangement to be sung, remember that singing for prayer is in a "normal" register, not an operatic or solo style. People may remain silent except for the responses, or they may lift up names of persons or situations related to each petition.

Silence (1 minute)

Leader: Hear the good news. If we confess our sins, God is faithful and just and will forgive us our sins and cleanse us from all unrighteousness. In the name of Jesus Christ, we are forgiven.
People: In the name of Jesus Christ, we are all forgiven.
All: Glory to God, *Amen*.

Lord's Prayer

Blessing

Leader: Let us go forth rejoicing in the strength of the Holy Spirit.
People: Thanks be to God.

The Peace

OBSERVATIONS AND FEEDBACK FOR WORSHIP LEADERS

Team Members:
Series/Seasonal Theme:
Service Theme:
Local Context:

Energy

Before Entrance: "Energy Challenge!" Attention and energy scattered in multiple directions
Entrance: Synchronizing the Assembly through Whole Body Actions
Word/Response: Active, Attentive Listening
Modes of Energy in Response(s): invitation, confessing faith, prayers, baptism, receiving members, and so on
Table: Confession, Pardon, Peace, Offering, Great Thanksgiving, Distribution, After Receiving
Sending: Active/Propulsion into the World

Presence*

Prayerfulness ("heavy on awe and mystery, light on answers and recipes")
Comfort in Your Own Skin
Confidence
Care with words ("when we do use words, make them really count")

Leadership

Engaging the *worshipers* in worship by embodying the energy and action needed for each movement and moment in worship—Entrance, Word/Response, Table, Sending

Flow

Minor Transitions—between elements within movements

Bearings—between movements

To Entrance:

Entrance to Word/Response:

Word/Response to Table:

Table to Sending:

*Source for categories and quotes: *Strong, Loving and Wise: Presiding in Liturgy* by Robert W. Hovda, (Liturgical Press, 1983), 34–35.

WHAT AFFECTS PERCEPTIONS OF WORSHIP?

[Space
    Ambience
Energy
    Pre]sence
Leadership
    Flow

BASIC PATTERN OF WORSHIP

ENTRANCE

The people gather in Christ's name and assemble themselves as Christ's body to begin their worship of God with praise and prayer.

PROCLAMATION AND RESPONSE

The scriptures are read and preached, and the people respond. During the readings, the responses may include psalms, songs, anthems, hymns, drama, or art. Responses to the sermon may include a call to discipleship, confession of faith, services of the baptismal covenant, and prayers for the church and the world.

THANKSGIVING AND COMMUNION

The people are invited to the Lord's table, confess their sin, receive pardon, embrace one another in the peace of Christ, and offer themselves in praise and thanksgiving, with gifts of bread and wine, for God's mighty acts of salvation. The people receive the broken bread and poured cup as the Body and Blood of Christ, and give thanks for all they have received.

SENDING FORTH

Having praised God, heard God's word, responded, and been fed at the Lord's table, the people are sent out into the world to live as Christ's body, redeemed by his blood, in the power of the Holy Spirit.

READINGS FOR ADVENT, YEAR C

First Sunday of Advent
Jeremiah 33:14-16
Psalm 25:1-10 (*UMH*, no. 756)
1 Thessalonians 3:9-13
Luke 21:25-36

Second Sunday of Advent
Malachi 3:1-4
Luke 1:68-79 (*UMH*, no. 208)
Philippians 1:3-11
Luke 3:1-6

Third Sunday of Advent
Zephaniah 3:14-20
Isaiah 12:2-6
Philippians 4:4-7
Luke 3:7-18

Fourth Sunday of Advent
Micah 5:2-5a
Luke 1:46b-55 (*UMH*, no. 199)
Hebrews 10:5-10
Luke 1:39-45

CPSIA information can be obtained
at www.ICGtesting.com
Printed in the USA
LVOW02s0303130216
474771LV00012B/36/P